A Trip To Gentle's World

UGO ELIZABETH

ISBN:9798844219979
ISBN-13:

DEDICATION

I dedicate this poem to the almighty **GOD** for inspiration and above all for the grace to be able to put my thoughts together.

To my parents **Mr.& Mrs. Ugo Thomas** For words of encouragement and for being very supportive to the very end, Also to my **siblings** and my best friend **Samuel** for being supportive in their own little ways, I see you guys.

CONTENTS

ACKNOWLEDGMENTS

I would like to thank PIN Unicross for giving me a platform to express myself. I would also like to sincerely thank my best friend and brother, Samuel for making sure I never quit writing even when I had a thousand reason to stop. I also would like to acknowledge Precious my girlfriend, for making sure my poem gets published. You all have special place in my Heart.

BLACK ROSE

Tears filled eyes.
Empty belles,
Unfulfilled promises,
Broken dreams,
That's the language of the street.

Death, the harbinger of pain,
Men, the harbinger of sorrow,
Society, the harbinger of inequality.

The poor masses are left broken,
In Tears,
Struggling for their daily bread.
All hope lost.
Eventually the weak one's die in the streets,
Even those as fragile as a rose.

In the end, there is no goodness left in the world.
Just like a black rose,
All empathy is gone,
Tears are all that is left.

WHAT IS LOVE?

What is love?

Is it the way my heart skips a beat when I hear your voice?
Or the way your smile lights up a room?
Is it the butterflies I feel in my stomach when I am around you?
Is it the giddy way I feel when I walk down the aisle with you?
Is that love?

Is it the feel our bodies with the stars as our audience?
Is it the empty promises from your sugar coated lips?
Is this what love is about?

I saw the signs but I ignored it.
I went into it blindly,
And then I lost myself
My trusting heart got shattered,
Ocean of tears coming down my face like waterfalls.
You said you love me.
But it only left a hollow feeling in my heart.

I am all alone now,
Hating my heart for being weak,
Devastated and broken
Repeated asking myself,

"What Is Love?"

TROUBLED SOUL

I am toxic to everyone
Including myself.
I am my own Achilles heel
I am my own poison.
Stay with me at your own risk
I will slowly drain the life out of you
Just the same way my life force is being drained.

I live with past memories of unhappiness,
Bitter romance and failed dreams.
Hope is gone.
All is left is an empty shell,
A piece of matter occupying space.

I spend my nights alone,
Because I am toxic to people.
Do not come close to me,
For I am like a parasitic virus,
I will drain the life out of you
Like I do myself

THE ME YOU SEE

Pictures capture the exact emotions we display,
Leaving us bare for empaths to read,
Memories engraved on paper'
Hearts left to reminiscence,
The passage of the soul too hooded to see,
Secrets too deep to be revealed.

You think you know me,
Many have believed such assumptious lies.
I am the me you see,
The me you don't believe exist.

I am the thorn you detest,
And the comfy wools you appreciate.
I am the nightmares you are terrified of,
And the sweet dreams you welcome.
I am the angel you long to see,
And the demon you avoid.
I am the rebel you disapprove of,
And the saint you accommodate.
I am as pretty as a rose
And as ugly as coal.

I am what you make me,
The lies and the truths,
I act accordingly.
I can be as cold as coldhearted and mean as they say,
Or be as warm and welcoming.
I am the me you see,
The picture you in your mind.

LIFE OF AN INTROVERT

Alone but the whole world is in my room,
Being inside seems safe.
Under the cover of my duvet, my safe heaven,
To keep out the cold emanating from outside.

Like a flower kept in a vase, I do not like being among the wild
My introvert nature keeps me company with my books,
Leaving my imaginations to run amok.

I'll rather be indoor than out with company
Fake smiles isn't something I appreciate.

In my room the world comes alive, like imaginations.

THE MONSTER SILENCE CREATED

She was bullied
Not by friends but family.
Night after night
Her pillow gets drenched
Tears she let fall freely,
To ease the pain in her heart.

She was bullied into silence,
Even tears became a taboo
She had no outlet,
Nothing to help anchor the pain,
Silence they wanted, silence she gave.
Silence, they say is golden,
This one begot a monster,
A monster with bottled up emotions,
A monster with pent up anger.

She utters no words,
She just smiles
That devilish grin
O how I wish you knew,
How mercilessly she has murdered you in her mind.
If imaginations could be real,
The streets will be littered with dead bodies,
Of people that bullied her into silence.

She was bullied into silence
And the monster in her grew.
There will be massacre,
When the beast eventually rises,
Heaven help those caught in its wake.
The silent one will become the vicious one,
The prey will become the apex predator.

IGNIS FATUUS

Hearing your voice every morning
Brings me peace and tears,
Like a lactose intolerant patient taking yogurt,
Alluring yet dangerous.

Like a fire lit in the storm
Your presence is quite comforting,
Like mctemple and a baby EU, strolling into the night,
Or little Sicily and chinonye with their escapades,
We talk through the night.
No worries, just squealing with excitement,
Gossiping about everything and nothing.

Regrettably, this is all in my head
An ignus fatuus in my imaginary universe.
For the record, I am not crazy,
Fantasyland seems more serene than reality,
No hypocrite, just ally

THE REASON WHY

The sun rises every morning,
Illuminating,
On both the feebleminded and the iron willed,
Giving one as well as the other chance to live.

Round and round , the clock goes,
Year in year out
You struggle with nothing to show for it.
Not for lack of trying
But from lack of motivation
From lack of vision
From lack of self-worth.

Life serves you a tasty dinner of frustration,
In a room of confusion.
Leaving you to go through a bowel of actual shit,
To figure out where you went wrong,
With you gasping for air, with your last
Cylinder of hope.

Hello,
Are you awake?
Are you afraid?
Are you tired of living in this world?
Why don't you find a reason to live?

Live, not because of society,
Live, not because of society,
Live, not because of your friends,
Be the reason why you live.

Be your own catalyst
Be your own inspiration,

Be your own success story.
Live,
For you.

CAGED,LIKE CINDERELLA

Till my fairy godmother comes to free me.
Dressed like a princess for a night
Dancing under the moonlight
Without a prince to share in my joy for freedom.

The music of my soul, making my feet hyper,
Rhythm coursing through my veins,
Like oxygen to my lungs.
Free but alas it is short lived.
The morning comes with its chains of despair,
And the keys thrown into the dungeon of silence

HEART BLEEDS

Experience, they say is a teacher
And a teacher has a heart of gold
A teacher is supposed to be kind.
But this lady called life,
Ever so merciless,
Has taught her a big lesson.

Her mind is in chaos,
While her face is ever full of smiles,
She can't come to terms with her troubles,
They wear her down daily,
Leaving her drained.
Her heart bleeds,
While her tearducts holds no tears.

She is tired but doesn't want to give up
This lady called life,
Ever so callous,
Has made her heart bleed.

ENCHANTED

Your eyes, a beauty to behold
Your voice, like a siren
Has enchanted me,
I am lost in your embrace.

I have been caught in the web of my fantasy.
Art in poetry has called me
And like a love struck fool
I harkened to her call.
Art has enchanted me,
Only, I am a willing victim.

MAMA AFRICA

Mama Africa,
Beautiful yet proud,
Rich in culture,
The envy of the world.
She does not even try to impress them,
She knows her worth.

She raised her children in love,
Never treating one better than the other.
Yet, they are always at loggerheads,
Fighting for supremacy.
They no longer stand united.

O mama Africa,
Your children have forgotten your training.
They have copied western ways,
And abandoned yours.
They have thrown caution in the wind,
They have brought war to themselves.

O mama Africa,
Peace have evaded your home.
Your little children are suffering,
Suffering from the mistakes of their fathers.
They are at the receiving end,
Receiving end of weapons of mass destruction,
Gotten from western education,
Losing parents at such tender ages.

O mama Africa,
Protect your little ones,
Teach them your old peaceful ways
Let love lead.

RAPE

It felt like a nightmare
Only this time it was real
I had read stories and heard the news
But I never thought it could happen to me.

It felt so wrong
There was nothing I could do
Crying out did not work
Nobody came to my rescue
When it was finally over, all I could do was cry.
I felt like trash
I kept asking myself how it happened.
My mind could not come to terms with what happened.

The pain never went away
The memories continued to haunt me.
To make matters worse, people blamed me.
"You should not have been out by that time"
"You know men cant control themselves"
"What were you wearing?"
Such statements kept breaking my spirit.

Eventually they all forgot,
All except me.
I still live with the memories,
Memories of that day.

BLACK OCTOBER

It stated like every other day.
Little did they know it would be their last.
Lights out, gunshots, bodies dropping like
Raindrops during a heaven rainfall.
Pandemonium broke out
My people have fallen
Killed by those meant to protect them.

It stated peacefully
The youths were no longer happy with the way things were.
They finally decided to drop their phones and fight
Fight for their rights
Fight for their voices to be heard
Little did they know that their country was
Under military rule using democracy as a guise

For the first time, I was proud to be called a Nigerian youth.
That day we decided to defy our parents
We stood together as one
No religion, tribe or ethnicity stood against us
We were unstoppable
They saw this and were afraid
So they decided to uproot the seed before it germinated.

We all will remember that day
Democracy died that day
Mother lost their children that day
It was indeed a black day in the month of October.
A part of us died that day
We will never forget.

THE AFRICAN STORY

The story of Africa I heard of
Were tales of lazy overfed humans.
People that needed to be taught a lesson,
A course on headwork.
The Africa I have come to know
Is full of hardship and suffering,
Even in the midst of plenty
The people get so little,
Struggling to survive in a continent
Where shackles of slavery mentality still holds us black.

I wonder the lesson they meant to teach us
When all I see is oil spilling from structures they forced upon us,
Putting us in a box too congested for even fishes to live in.
Every morning we breathe in air of false hope,
Wishing things would get better
Yet silently expecting the worst.
How could we dare to dream big
When even our brethren's looked us in the eyes
And trapped our souls in a pandora box set
For a voyage to the underworld , a place of no return.
Just for a few shillings and enough drinks to fill their belles.

The Africa story is a peculiar one,
Filled with anguish, despair and of course fear,
Fear of the unknown.
Now we acclaim that we are free
But still addicted to the whips
Living a life without dignity and pride,
While we suffering and smile under their

ABOUT THE AUTHOR

Ugo Elizabeth is a Nigerian from Imo State and a Student of Cross Rivers University Of Technology, in the Department Of Plant Science And Biotechnology. She is an ambivert that is outspoken and friendly. She is a member of Poets Initiative Of Nigeria, Unicross chapter. This is her first published poem book.

www.ingramcontent.com/pod-product-compliance
Lightning Source LLC
Chambersburg PA
CBHW071259140726
47996CB00007B/2904